Hypnotizing Lines

also by j.d.tulloch

Undiscovered Paladins: Westward Rhymes Revisited
(39 West Press 2015)

Neutral Receding Lines: Road Rhymes, Volume Two
(39 West Press 2013)

The Will to Resist: and psalms of anger, love & humanity
(39 West Press 2010)

edited by j.d.tulloch

Desolate Country: We the Poets, United, Against Trump
(39 West Press 2017)

Prompts! A Spontaneous Anthology
(39 West Press 2016)

Hypnotizing Lines

Road Rhymes, Volume One

j.d.tulloch

39 WEST
PRESS

39 WEST PRESS
Kansas City, MO
www.39WestPress.com

Copyright © 2011 by j.d.tulloch

All rights reserved. No part of this book may be reproduced, scanned, or distributed in any printed or electronic form, including information storage and retrieval systems, without permission. Please do not participate in or encourage piracy of copyrighted materials in violation of the author's rights. Please purchase only authorized editions.

First Edition: August 2011

ISBN: 978-0-615-52220-3

Library of Congress Control Number: 2011935808

This book is a work of fiction. Names, characters, places, dates, and incidents are products of the author's imagination, or are used fictitiously, satirically, or as parody. Any resemblance to actual persons, living or dead, business establishments, events, or locales is entirely coincidental.

10 9 8 7 6 5 4 3 2

Design, Layout, Front Cover Photo: j.d.tulloch

39WP-05A

CONTENTS

Prologue i

Volume One

Hypnotized 5
Jesus & The Church of Malt Liquor 8
Progression in G(A) Minor 9
Ostensibly: Ogden 10
Wired 11
At Last 13
Circuit Board Blues 15
Lasciate ogne speranza, voi ch'intrate. 17
Mephistopheles, the Hustler & a Gyro 18
Sunday in Portland OR: Sue Me George Lucas 19
(Properly) Not a Poem 20
Again 21
Pleeeeethora 22
Big Tree 23
Keep Right 24
INflatiON 25
Missing the Beat 26
Soon Wilshire Soon 30
Past Palisades Park 32
Meanwhile I-($%#@&) 33
L.A. Breakfast with a Professor, Retired 34
Contentious Clouds 35
Rhymes of Ancient Mariners 37
Hounds of Hell 39
Log Cabin Lament 40
Superstition Ain't the Way 41
My Turn 42
Valleys of Fire 44
Converging 46
HOT SEXY GIRLS 48
The Heart of the Coconut 51
Chasing Ghosts 52

BURNING OCEAN	54
SOMEWHERE	56
HE AIN'T HEAVY; HE'S MY BROTHER	57
MELODY #87	60
DIZZY MATH (THE THIZZ OF NATURE)	62
DARK AGES	63
THE RACE	64
THE TRUTH (FROM A HOTEL ROOM IN FLAGSTAFF)	66
BECOMING	67
TURN AROUND	69
)E-M-O-H(	71
HIATUS: OF	72

PROLOGUE

She is as good as new and ready to hit the road on what might be her final curtain call: one last gest—a cross-country pilgrimage—to both lands unseen and destinations revisited. *The Lincoln* (my reliable traveling companion), restored within the confines of a limited budget and (*mostly*) reborn to her original 1997 glory, embarked with me on what has evolved into a twenty-thousand-plus mile journey of self-exploration and discovery, seeking not necessarily more fruitful pastures but rather trekking westward—and then eastward—on a noble quest of inspiration, an escapade of adventure, in search of an *American Dream* that once hearkened the spirits of forgotten voyagers who beckoned me from afar as Horace Greeley loudly whispered in my ear, "Go west, young man ... Go west."

• • • • • • • • • • • •

Blank stares populate the faces of what Emory University English Professor Mark Bauerlein dubs "The Dumbest Generation," the fifty million "diverted, distracted, and devoured" minds of Millennials and Echo Boomers who represent Generation Y, The Google Generation, or Gen Net.

But Bauerlein's labeling of only Millennials as "The Dumbest Generation" expresses a short-sided world view and a misplaced condemnation of only a small percentage of the over 750 million global adherents to the Facebook Fad, a peer-pressure driven social networking culture of assimilation that distracts users from the realities of the world and focuses attentions on interpersonal social dramas while devouring thoughts with unnecessary obsessions that revolve entirely around knowing exactly what online "friends" are up to (and thinking about) each minute of the day.

"The Dumbest Generation" should be defined more accurately to include all passive participants of *The Information Age*, representing, therefore, a trans-generational phenomenon—aptly referred to here as *The Borg Generation* (apologetically borrowed from the *Star Trek* antagonist comprised of a hive of assimilated drones)—where citizens of all ages plug into a global collective of electronic voyeurism and narcissism that in essence merely projects to others a false sense of one's own importance and standing in the world through superficial status updates, wall posts, instant and text messages, and one-hundred forty character tweets, creating slangs of reduced vocabulary while eliminating complex thought, abolishing insightful reflection, and reducing articulate prose to the lowest common denominator, forever trapping the majority of partakers in a prison of postponed social and cerebral development.

Today, we stand at the edge of an intellectual, cultural, and economic crisis. While information is more readily available to *The Borg Generation* than to any previous generation since the advent of writing in the fourth millennium BCE, more and more prisoners willfully sit shackled in the *darkness* of Plato's cave (*The Republic: Book VII*) and consequently remain unenlightened concerning basic scientific, political and historical facts. Therefore, the real test of our survival and continued evolution as a cognizant people hinges on our ability to correctly use and disseminate accurate and constructive information—like we have seen in the social-media-led revolutions in Tunisia and Egypt—via the au courant technological might that sits freely at our disposal.

In the mid-fifteenth century, those in power saw Guttenberg's movable type printing press and subsequent distribution of one-hundred eighty Bibles as the potential bastion of downfall of elite control over the masses: knowledge is power. In many ways, that new medium of communicating information on a broader scale facilitated the mainstreaming—not commercialization—of counter-culture and allowed novel ideas that contradicted archaic thought to spread amongst the multitudes, thereby creating a Renaissance of science, art, and literacy.

To many, however, the printing press seems outdated by today's technological standards. With a computer—or smart phone—and an Internet connection, any global citizen can potentially reach far more *blank* minds than Guttenberg's Bible ever did. The capacity of the World Wide Web to invoke positive change is awesome, but at the same time, distraction runs amok on the Internet by virtue of social networking sites that latently create a false realities by promoting the propagation of worthless information, e.g., when your co-worker last had a bowel movement, needlessly distracting us from the worthwhile information that actually affects our daily lives.

• • • • • • • • • • • •

While sipping lukewarm coffee in a sterile Internet café and reflecting upon where my travels with *The Lincoln* have led me, it would be presumptuous to assume that a printed book of road musings masquerading as poems qualifies as worthwhile information, but I do, however, hope my words from the road arouse the contagion of inspiration in the hearts and minds of in-the-know artists, actors, and activists; singers, songwriters, and musicians; painters, filmmakers, and writers; and independent entrepreneurs and business owners who, through simply saying "no," choose to transcend the control of mainstream corporate, capitalist ideology and instead strive to create a self-realized American Dream of know how vis-à-vis self-explorative creative, artistic, and transparent commercial endeavors that selflessly serve to uplift the majority of humanity rather than further facilitating the advancement and concentration of wealth of the minority of individuals and immortal corporations who economically enslave us all.

We must stand together, and apart, in unison and discord, as a generation of knowing individuals whose ideas and ideals aim to focus our collective energies on social change rather than social networking, on tearing down walls rather than posting gossip to them, and on fostering face to face connections rather than facebooking from afar, thus sowing the seeds of a twenty-first century renaissance where each individual embraces an empathetic existential freedom and embarks on a voyage of self-discovery that immediately seizes life and unselfishly makes the most of each opportunity by putting the shared needs of humankind first and the self-centered desires of the individual last. Our survival depends upon it. Welcome to the k(no)w ...

Volume One

"I find it wholesome to be alone the greater part of the time. To be in company, even with the best, is soon wearisome and dissipating ... I never found the companion that was so companionable as solitude."

Henry David Thoreau
Walden (1854)

HYPNOTIZED

      Rolling—
Kansas Flint Hills
Natural prairie land
Of majesty tenders endless
Puissance, supply: windmill farms
Arising from the abyss of eternity
Prodigious pallid turbines litter
The landscape surrenders
To the (green) generation
Of clean renewable energy
Courtesy the territory's
Power-providing monopoly.

      Hypnotizing lines repeat continuously,
mile after mile, guiding travel.

      Broadcasting—
Thermometer's sturdy
102 yields not
The cabin of *The Lincoln* survives
A sanguine struggle to keep cool
Food and fuel anticipate
Hays' relocated Rome
Buffalo roam
Bill Cody's defunct
Cholera-plagued home
On the range
Now estranged
From home
The Home
I no longer
Know a thirst to
Exchange Midwest heat for
Sweet mountain breeze.

      Billowing—
Boulder's streets dominate
Rockies' reflection
At sunset red glare
Interstate-70 wears
Heavy splattered insects litter
The windshield buries
Minute life succumbing
Tragically seared by
A slab of safety glass soaring
Through anonymous air
Caskets at seventy-two.

      Hypnotizing lines repeat, continuously,
      mile after mile, guiding arrival.

      Riding—
Cyclists bank on
Bike lanes running
Parallel city roads proffer
Parking racks galore evoke
Berkeley East

(Green) eco
Friendly buses burn
Clean diesel transports
Scores down town
Pedestrian traffic dominates
Street theatre prevails.

LEFT: Slow-motion mimes chase imaginary poisonous arrows like Cupid trying to reclaim a misfire, an ill-conceived match destined for failure.

RIGHT: Sleight of hand magicians deceive onlookers, momentarily sidetracking shoppers searching for sizzling sales at trendy boutiques.

FRONT: A juggler twirls sticks of fire, a sideshow distraction to a musician magically plucking his semi-acoustic guitar in unison with a stale carnival keyboard.

BACK: An out of place suit screams out the disastrous details of his tee time tomorrow, insisting that his voice be heard above the rest.

SIDE: A non-metered sprinter swiftly passes by carrying a forlorn fare piggy-back style.

OUT: I am surrounded alone

        (unseen)

    Hypnotizing lines repeat continuously,
    mile after mile, beckoning sweet mountain breeze
    guiding me down the street.

Jesus & The Church of Malt Liquor

a trinity of dirty hippies
       (with nothing but a bongo)
             mistakes my
                   rolled fag
                        for a spliff.

a congregation of thirty tourists
       (with nothing but green)
             mistakes the
                   paroled stags
                        for riffraff.

de jesus of sturdy boulder
       (with nothing but *songo*)
            mistakes his)
                   $(old scags
                        for a fatted calf.

a tea party of quirky white-breads
       (with nothing but sheen)
             mistakes their
                   gold bags
                        for the staff of life.

a dirty hippie was Jesus & The Church of Malt Liquor
now accepts donations, change with a promise:
collections purchase nothing but booze: salvation.

Progression in G(A) Minor

befogged by daybreak's dawn like a fawn confronting
first light upon deserting her mother's womb, the
asphalt amuses as if the Colorado State Police were

on my t(r)ail. the Wyoming line could not sooner
consummate my relationship with US-287, but Fort
Collins' sprawl slows my descent to a rapid crawl.

caffeine dreams' wired nightmares mar patience—
delayed, like a refugee seeking safe access through
over around under The *Great* Mexican Wall, only to

be held by an after-market governor restricting
Time's precarious passage. at last, unmolested
advance, but Laramie re-sounds Matthew Shepard's

closeted cry. like a ghostly mist i flee silent
symphonies carelessly composed by hayseed
sociopaths and advance on a path where broken

mountains marry hodgepodge plains' crescendoing
plateaus with out objection from traditional foes.
faraway from somewhere (nowhere better explains),

i survive
as the conveys of slower soldiers to my right
expire in the night.

i progress
as the solitary soldier
is martyred in the night.

Ostensibly: Ogden

       i'm told
       Two-Bit Street
       was too seedy for
       Al Capone:

illicit street gambling walking narcotics bootleggers trafficking
refuge supplied by
speakeasies
safe Sanctuary

       i'm told
       Two-Bit Street
       was tamed by
       Mormons:

twenty till ten tattoo parlor padlocked Tabernacle trafficking
refuge supplied by
a single saloon
speak-easing
soloed songs slamming
abuse cantos of latter day obsessions emitting
patchoulied sounds indistinct odors reeking
staled cigars resonating
proverbial open-miked coffee shops pinching
joseph smith's wives rebirthing
the guarantee of
safe sanctuary

       i'm told
       Two-Bit Street
       was too seedy for
       Al Capone:

secure Alcatraz isle
supplies
safer Sanctuary

WIRED

                 halfway
to the North Pole
mainlined adrenaline courses
coasting veins downward
      effortlessly
           descending
                  the 45th parallel

injecting six degree declines
build momentum
      gallantly
           sailing

at extraneous speeds of
eighty p
     l
    u
     m
      m
       e
        t
         i
          n
           g
like eight Mark VIII torpedoes
h u n t i n g targets unseen

      swiftly
streets akin
to Nice
present delusions
of formula one
submersibles racing
                p u m p i n g

popping ears
compress
      c o m p e t i n g
          to sustain sea-lagged cylinders

Idaho sinks sunset
Oregon cascades
hazard lights ahead of
green forest air inhaled in
synonymous breaths with
fresh Danish shag

waiting submissively
    (wasting)
as the slug impeding procession
creeps onward in the rayless
dimness of dominate dusk

waiting aggressively
    (basting)
as Portland's radiance
emerges from the ray less
dominance of dusk

At Last

Skidmore fountain reflects skid row: a one-armed vagabond serves the soundtrack for the day's festivities, painting abstract portraits of Willie Nelson while delicately strumming banging flat-picking raping caressing the neck of his jaded guitar with a splayed wooden stick deftly affixed to the nub of his right arm.

A dollar bill escapes my front pocket and easily squats shelter in his tip jar—an upside-down ten-gallon Stetson—summoning a later cause for celebration as discovery of my ~~generosity~~ blunder sends him twenty reasons to continue entertaining.

Not wanting to be upstaged, a pewter statue dances to life and slowly shifts from stoic Moses to dying Gaul, startling a small child, unaware that the sham stone sculpture stinks charlatan: an out-of-work actor layered with pounds of silver make-up in perfect disguise.

Twin glass towers mount whiskey river banks, ripping currents through the Saturday market that resemble the sounds of shells firing from an AK-47, but no need for panic as a German tourist sporting a brand-new SLR camera is spotted snapping hundreds of shots of his six-year-old daughter in a split-second.

Cosseted under the shade of an English elm, a dread-locked hippie sits sketching a charcoal drawing of the homeless man sleeping silently on the fading lawn in front of him, both ignorant of adjacent tent city's bustling peddler's paradise populated by active artists hocking hand-crafted wares: merchandise manufactured and marketed with the hope of maintaining a bohemian lifestyle.

With a heaping plate of Himalayan in hand, West Wind wrestles the water below and whips the promenade repeatedly, rhythmically fashioning a soothing zephyr that wafts the halfzware shag from my hemp paper, percolating the

implausibility of rolling the perfect smoke or consuming curry
  dumplings lentils rice green beans potatoes tomatoes
  cucumbers in blissful ardor.

But—
  My hunger pains wait.
  My nicotine fix waits.

From its unselfish flowing fountain,
  surfeited skid row serves something recycled:
  a serendipitous slice of self-determination.

Ingesting my own sovereignty
  I am.

  I am (free)
  at last.

Circuit Board Blues

Echo's forlorn cries ricochet from the glens,
        prophetically project soothing sounds
        through the æther that reverberate in
        the depths of consciousness, reflect the
        almighty authority of the ocean, and
        surreptitiously summon me to the sea.

Portland daytrippers maraud along the highway
        in hybrid chariots and descend like
        medieval Norse Vikings invading Cannon
        Beach's reticent settlement, pilfering
        every dry dock within beach's reach.

Low lying clouds imitate the colour of The Deep
        and merge with the horizon, fusing sky's
        end and the beginning of Poseidon's realm.

Haystack Rock and her twin needled companions
        protrude from the brine and remind me
        where my self-imposed banishment began
        miles down beach's end.

High tide delivers a solitary surfer who catches
        a right and cross-steps down the deck of
        his longboard before needlessly grubbing.

A pending tempest produces no magnificent sunset
        today, but the fresh fragrance of the ocean
        wind sends chills down my spine as my spirit
        skyrockets over my body into the clouds
        above and back down to the waves below.

Instantly—
        all thoughts flee my head in a meditative
        state of holy supreme euphoric dystopia.

Momentarily—
    I stop breathing (and my heart ceases
    beating) while duality direct dials me
    into the circuit board's broadband modem
    of universal connectivity.

Simultaneously—
    I am
    snorkeling the coral reefs of the Great Guana Cay
    sculling the quick waters of the muddy Missouri
    sinking into the snow white sands of Pensacola Beach
    motoring a nameless lake after pirating a clipper
    commuting by express boat down the Chao Phraya
    skiffing in the Gulf of Mexico outside New Orleans
    surfing Ocean Beach breakers right of the jetty
    captaining a sailboat in a regatta in Mobile Bay
    arriving via schooner into Victoria Harbour at sunset.

Tragically—
    I am
    satisfied
        content
            at peace

Eternally—
    I am
    you
        (are me)
            we are
                here

                    I wish
                    you
                    were
                    here.

Lasciate ogne speranza, voi ch'intrate.

Downtown Portland bustles pedestrian passengers:
        colonies of army ants
        vacating the district
        for asylum in suburban
        hills after collecting
        daily supplies
        of pests
        from *en masse*
        column raids.

City Center spits out a mob of migrant middlemen:
        swarms of worker bees
        fleeing the urban core
        for asylum in suburban
        hives after collecting
        daily supplies
        of pollen
        from flowering
        office cubicles.

Dusk dawns a nocturnal crew of culture's underbelly:
        canvassing clans of homeless hippies
        (with pan flutes and bongo drums)
        staking claims
        to urban street corners
        and panhandling for currency
        like Pavlovian puppies
        pleading for treats
        from enabling masters.

Oh Virgil! Guide me through this fiery Inferno.
        Protect me from Geryon's treachery and deceit.
        And I promise not to ditch you in Purgatorio.

Mephistopheles, the Hustler & a Gyro

Mephistopheles traps me at the bar
   While sipping Goldschläger from a snifter,
   And thus commences our shibboleth spar.

Assuming I'm nothing but a drifter,
   The ponytailed shrink starts his assessment;
   So, I swiftly don the role of grifter.

A two-buck beer his lofty investment,
   But his rhapsodic rants fail to amuse
   As does his plea for my shirt's divestment.

Loaded with piety and full of booze,
   I flee Silverado for the dank street
   In search of a surrogate muse to schmooze.

On the concrete looms impending repeat:
   A sobbing hustler swapping sex bizarre.
   I hastily flee his web of deceit,

   But he pursues me to the dining car.
   I gift a gyro and say *au revoir*.

Sunday in Portland OR: Sue Me George Lucas

Beyoncé, Sweetie Pie,
and the slightly evil Bugsy
   (innocently)
peck at my feet

Anakin
   (patiently)
mans the flames
of the barbecue

Princess Leia
   (reluctantly)
remains skeptical
of her inflatable pool

Queen Amidala
   (diligently)
searches the backyard
for freshly laid chicken eggs

Has heaven reared its ugly head?

NO—

Portland Sunday
   (intentionally)
sows the seeds
of trademark infringement

OR:

Sue me George Lucas

(Properly) Not a Poem

                Friends engage in mass Diaspora,
                   spreading themselves thin
                     across the land like
                      earth's inhabitants
                       after Babel's
                           fall.

Instagram Facebook Twitter texts Four-Square connects.

                           Letters
                        lost smiling
                     at strangers on
               sidewalk trash littering
            street curb transgressions
         denying forgiveness bottled zones
      comforting perspiration bonging fast
food seeking guitar bass trumpets contagion.

                                          Inspiration.

(Properly)

                        future

Again

Juliet said to Romeo:
PARTING IS SUCH SWEET SORROW.

But de-parting Portland
and venturing down
the California coast
I refuse to say ~~goodbye~~
         adiós to my friends.

Goodbye exists for eternity—
like writing your name
in freshly poured concrete:
immortalized for perpetuity
on the Grecian Urn of Time
for all of humanity to see.

Instead—
I ephemerally inscribe
UNTIL WE MEET AGAIN
on the wet sands
of a beach
somewhere near
Crescent City.

By the time
the fleeting tide
crashes ashore
and washes away
the sentiment,
I will have returned
from the sea
to see
you
again.

Pleeeeeethora

SOUTH
down *The 101*

ODYSSEY
into Humboldt County

primordial ooze
impregnates my quintessence

the smell of KB
loads my lungs
with unsullied ocean ozone
filling them to capacity
like ignited propane gas
expelling super-heated air
inflating the envelope
of a hot air balloon

moments before
its thin epidermal layer RU P T U   R   E   S
i relax

the sensation
sweeps through my soul
like the morning dew
passing through
the canopy of
any
RED
wood
park
randomly discovered
by the mapping service
of a popular Internet
~~search engine~~ data miner

Big Tree

timeless trees scrape the skyline,
shading squadrons of safarists
from scintillating summer sun.

Big Tree audaciously ascends from
California soil into the stratosphere,
invading Zeus' sphere of influence

and angering him enough to send
clear-cutters to the realm below,
punishing the titanic trees for hubris.

but Gaia intervenes, saving
the redwood groves for her
enervated earth children.

rings later—

regal redwoods assume their rightful
thrones with divine right proudly project
wisdom's power to their forest subjects.

it's safe out here, secluded from
the city (protected from the
elements) by my redwood rulers.

it's nice out here, protected from
the city (secluded from the
elements) by the ruling redwoods.

i think i'll lumber
                around
                              the lumber and timber.

Keep Right

California road signs exclaim:
   SLOWER TRAFFIC KEEP RIGHT

Oregonian drivers tread
into California proceed
ignorant to advice carry on
refuse to yield to faster vehicles

Portland's political correctness amok proclaims:
   DO NOT PUMP PETROL
   DO NOT PICK UP PILGRIM PASSENGERS
   DO NOT PONTIFICATE ON A PHONE WHILE POUNDING THE PAVEMENT
   PLEASE POSSESS POT FOR PERSONAL PUTREFACTION

Cosmos whispers to searching shepherds:
  tap high a dormant keg
  awake like Goldilocks a hibernating bear

                                         (redemption)

  spawn common courtesy
  shun selfish deeds
  seamlessly merge into the alliance of awareness

    &

  altruistically allow those
  on/in a different (p)lane
  to pass freely into obscurity

INFLATION

Penny a thoughT
Five a baR
Ten a poinT
Twenty a rolL
Thirty a thirtY
Sixty an eightH
One-twenty a balL

$x = (-b \pm \sqrt{(b^2 - 4ac)})/2a$

StimulatioN
        O
       i
      t
     a
    l
   f
  N
 I

Missing the Beat

the free way ends
and i pay the six dollar toll
cross the Golden Gate
but arrive in San Francisco
a few generations too late

Renaissance drums no longer *Beat*
Janis Joplin's counter-culture
cry of freedom no longer reverberates
throughout *The Haight's*
gentrified neighborhood
head shops record stores bars pubs
try to recapture the Summer of Love

Renaissance drums no longer beat
Harvey Milk's counter-culture
plea of equality no longer burrows
throughout *The Castro's*
gentrified neighborhood
token rainbow flags proudly fly
over drunken drag queens
leading street parades on their knees

William Carlos Williams provided—
        no letter of introduction
        no lsdpcpghbmdma to expand my consciousness
        no place to stay in the City by the Bay

    where (like Ginsberg)
  i too
have seen
my peers
STARVING HYSTERICAL NAKED
chasing the (white) dragon before
fixing themselves

to the temporary tempo
of a slowed drum circle
(a retarded circadian rhythm)

    where (like Ginsberg)
 i too
have seen
suburban junkies
DESTROYED BY MADNESS
languishing couch-ridden
in pharmaceutical comas before
dying slowly in depressing drug den
living rooms of low-end
providers! dealers! servers! of life's hope

    where (like Ginsberg)
 i too
have seen
VISIONS! OMENS! HALLUCINATIONS! MIRACLES! ECSTASIES!
or
more likely
certainties. axioms. palpabilities. mediocrities. miseries.

    and

    where (like Ginsberg)
 i too
am with you

 i too
am with you
in North Beach
crying chaos with Ferlinghetti

 i too
am with you
in the Tenderloin
trying madly not to succumb

   i too
am with you
in Mid-Market
being swept off the street

   i too
am with you
in the Mission
demurring the oppressive Ellis Act

   i too
am with you
in the Mission
serving coffee not the cops

   i too
am with you
in the Mission
dodging the Google mastodons

   i too
am with you
on the Embarcadero
expiring in gridlock aborting time

   i too
am with you
at the Ferry Building's clock tower
snapping photos capturing time

   i too
am with you
at Rincon Park
eating lunch from a brown paper bag

   i too
am with you
in the shadow of Cupid's Span
standing as a martyr

(to the place where
Tony Bennett left his heart)

  i too
am with you
on the Bay Bridge
stretching across the sea for eternity

  i too
am with you
on *The 80, 580*, and *5*
California ground

  i too
am with you
as i amicably depart San Francisco
L.A. bound

but i think i'll
take my punctured
bleeding heart
with me

it
may come in handy
somewhere
down the road

my still beating heart
may come in handy
down the road

Soon Wilshire Soon

carefree road runners soar
down *The 5* in search of Angels
until Wile E. Coyote intervenes

with an Acme explosive,
transforming the tactile tract of
tar into a paved parkwaying lot

overrun by sedentary snails.
(California traffic travels at two
 tempos: 186,000 miles per

second or absolute atrophy.)
speed limit signs vanish into the
void, scratched from roadsides

and terminated like the T-1000
by the Gubernator('s budget
cuts). commuters clog the San

Diego Freeway, firing fossil fuels
and wasting treasures of time in
traffic. held captive against my

will—a slave to the city's daily
demands—my patience grows
thin as saltwater dreams

detonate my dome, sending
signals of secession to the sacra
at the base of my spine.

waiting
for Wilshire Boulevard,
waiting.

sneaking
forward, slowly
sneaking.

closing
on my target, casually
closing

(like a battalion
of foot soldiers creeping across
Settentrione).

retreating,
not today:
proceeding.

Wilshire will soon
supervise my passage
to the sea.

soon, Wilshire will
shepherd
the sea unto me.

Past Palisades Park

Palisades Park pushes me over stony scarps
onto a pedestrian passageway that spans the PCH,
sending me the sands of Santa Monica Beach.

Subterranean sapphire saliva disguises
cloudless azure skies; snow-white
caps collide with strand's shallow shore.

Schools of social sharks stride up and down
and down and up the seaboard, savoring
a summer stroll of superfluous satisfaction.

Sunbathers sit subservient to Sun's smile,
slowly scorching their spotted sheaths,
unscathed by the seething scarlet stains.

Surfers assemble side-by-side; soon, the
looming swell will surface and scores
of stoked Slaters will step into liquid.

Suddenly, a sundry of seraphim schlepps me
to Svarga, sentencing me to a stretch of satiety
superior to any subsequent metempsychosis.

So, I surf out past the breakers,
leave the past behind.

Out past the breakers,
the past passes away.

Meanwhile i-($%#@&)

Meanwhile, in beautiful downtown Burbank …

A major multimedia megacorporation
      —managed
      by a mickey mouse
      mostly possessed
      by the fruity man
      promising
      the latest i-($%#@&) airminipluNsproretina device—
bombards America's adolescents
with pre-fabricated pop ~~star~~starts
that grow up to be
tina smoking nude posing
drunk driving *yeyo* snorting
head shaving rehab living
bulimic petty addictive
thieves.

With other directors
in unison he screams:

CAPTURE THE CHILDREN.
HOMOGENIZE THEIR HEADS.
CONCOCT A CULTURE OF CONSUMERS.

With sane defectors
in dissension I scream:

DREAMS DO NOT COME TRUE AT THEME PARKS.

Meanwhile, in beautiful downtown Burbank.

L.A. Breakfast with a Professor, Retired

at nine, L.A.
time, *Times* in hand,
the retired professor
sits alone at
the kitchen table
taking breakfast.
i quietly join him.

turning the page,
the byline
storyline
timeline
provides fodder:
ruminative fare.
Rousseau was a Marxist.

with the slapdash
zeal of a child,
he hurriedly
bites into
a slice of
cherry pie.
i eagerly join him

Contentious Clouds

the mild Santa Monica sun
(guaranteed to the masses)
again lures me seaside.
before advancing onward,
my civic responsibility
requires me once more
to rollick
under Sol's gaseous glory.

Neptune majestically molds
a mild serf
while Hyperion upholds
his covalent covenant
with California
chargés d'affaires,
granting yet another day
of idiosyncratic elegance

to the multitudes.
in a twist of fate
(patently part of
the pact to provide
unprecedented pulchritude),
Disney ironically
co-opts Hyperion's handle
to promote its imprint

of bestselling books
to bairn demographics.
crossroads aside,
spreading solicitude
suddenly swells
straight through
my substance,
surrounding me

like sub-atomic positrons
circling the nucleus
of a hydrogen isotope
seconds after
the cyclopean explosion
of a singularity.
through friction,
Helios carefully

commands his chariot
across the sky,
skillfully steering
setting sun
as it disappears
on the horizon
and descends
into the sea,

delivering darkness
until tomorrow's dawn
and the leading rays
of the new-fangled
reborn sun.
contentious clouds
no longer hover
into my heart

to deliver
a deluge
of precipitation
but arise from oblivion,
adding a magnanimous stain
to my sunset sky.
clouds arise from oblivion
and magnanimously stain

my sunset sky.

Rhymes of Ancient Mariners

Spartan scouts assemble by the sea,
Singing a paean to Poseidon.

Alexander pauses by the shore,
Sights silhouettes of brazen-hoofed horses

With manes of gold
Galloping across the skyline.

Rhymes of ancient Mariners
Resolutely ring from the Pacific's depths

And evaporate into the celestial sphere,
Delicately dancing across the atmosphere.

Condensating! Sublimating! Precipitating!
Delivering drops of life

Back down into the nadirs below.
In another gulf of time ...

Alexander pauses by the shore,
Sights brazen, black blankets of muck

Leaving behind a plume of rogue, deepwater droplets
Stretching mile after mile,

Refusing to dissipate
Despite deadly dispersants.

American addicts assemble by the sea,
Singing a paean to BP.

Rhymes of ancient Mariners
Resolutely ring from the Gulf's depths

And transform into tears of distress,
Dangerously dancing across the atmosphere.

Condensating. Sublimating. Precipitating.
Delivering sorrows of abuse

Back down into the nadirs below.
In time ...

Alexander pauses by the shore once more,
Sights silhouettes of brazen, liquid waves

Crashing into Sunset Cliffs
(With power unsurpassed).

High tides! Low tides! Riptides! A jetty!
Swells that reach far and vast.

Spartans come and addicts go,
Turn their backs on spiritual serenity,

Yet unconditionally it gives,
Freely gives of all its energy:

A love that is there for the taking,
A precious gift for all to share,

Rhymes of ancient Mariners
Resolutely ring, sing cries from the deep,

I AM THE OCEAN,
REACH OUT TO ME IF YOU DARE.

I *am* the ocean,
Reach out to *me* if you dare.

HOUNDS OF HELL

Reluctantly readying myself for the weariness of the way ahead, I already regret exchanging the ocean's brisk breath, the comforts of the coastal sun, and my bucolic beach-bum life(style) for the rigidly relentless desert heat and sweltering summer sky.

Scorching western sun chases me like the Hounds of Hell hawking heathens through the Wild Hunt in Wistman's Wood.

Pushing onward, I compete not only with calefaction but also U.S. Border Patrol checkpoints—Fourth Amendment-Free Zones—near the Mexican border on Interstate-8 as temperatures in the Sonoran peak at 110 and federal agents subject all travelers to warrantless searches, sniffing out *illegal* drugs (and aliens).

Reports of the detention of *patients*, the confiscation of *medicine*, and the prosecution of federal drug charges surface, despite President Obama's promise not to pursue cases against medical marijuana beneficiaries.

Predator drones protect borders but homeland security does not protect against UNREASONABLE SEARCHES AND SEIZURES.

Frightened by my quickly eroding civil liberties,
I flee the hounds of hell.

I fly.

Log Cabin Lament

The temperature smacks one-fifteen
In degrees of dry desert sheen.
   Air is thin but thick as well;
   I do believe this is hell.
Perhaps it's just the Benzedrine.

Giant saguaro flips me off,
With middle finger he doth scoff.
   His evil eyes follow me
   Through sands of iniquity,
Like Humbert Humbert. Nabokov!

Hold on. Listen. What do you hear?
That voice—its message—isn't clear.
   Some thing, some thing, the Lord's Prayer,
   Something to eat, drink, and wear
Bleeds F.M. Christ from speaker's ear.

Do not worry, Scottsdale is near.
Promises of two-for-one beer
   Ease silent thoughts of despair
   And guide me to Satan's lair,
Where Log Cabin spells hidebound queer.

Superstition Ain't the Way

Newspaper headlines warn of danger here:
Missing hiker found near Lost Dutchman trail.
Thar's gold in them thar hills foretells folktale,
So near Superstition explorers leer
In search of treasure; dreams of wealth appear.
Coronado heeds not Thunder God's rail
Against transgressing sacred grounds' safe swale;
Soon, decapitated, ugly heads rear.
Here, newspaper headlines warn of danger:
Three hikers hunting lost treasure feared dead.
Bygone ghosts of ancestors bleed blood red
And, dying, declare life's final mission:
Belief in Superstition leads, stranger,
To the belief in more superstition.

My Turn

Scottsdale's suffocating sweat
sends me somewhere uncertain:

scintillating Sedona and Grand
Canyon's skywalk or straight to

Sin City. substantially spent (and
slightly spinning) from Saturday's

shenanigans, a sabbatical from
the asphalt would be sublime, but

my Scottsdale savior prefers to
spend Sunday in solitude. not

wanting to overstay my welcome
in the land of Log Cabin and

Goldwater Republicans,
i saunter alone through

Scottsdale's streets before
halfheartedly setting sail for

Vegas, saving the surrendered
seas of the Grand Canyon for

another day. saffron plasma sun
sets atop Hualapai Mountains on

US Route 93. in nearby Kingman,
three inmates escape Arizona's

prison state. unaccompanied by
darkness, i, a-part with the road,

share only pensive thoughts of
freedom with myself and the

cosmos. lessons of Jean-Paul
Sartre traipse the dun fantastic: a

reminder that we—alone on this
rock—are condemned to be free

with no other destinies than the
ones we forge ourselves. nearing

the microcosm of American
gluttony, Hoover Dam weeps;

neon perennials bloom, arising
from valley heights. a solitary tear

escapes my wearied eye, softly
rolling down my unshaven cheek.

the Strip leaves me speechless,
searching for suitable words

(asking myself),
IS IT MY TURN NOW?

(answering myself)
now, it's my turn.

Valleys of Fire

unrestrained independence awakes
my conscious mind exudes instant
ecstasies understood only by my
subconscious. swiftly fleeing the

security of my bedsheets, outside
cloudless sky leaves unrestrained sun
sending boiling beams of ultraviolet
radiance to the torrid terra firma,

superheating the cement wasteland
of desert sprawl. khaki stucco houses
parody pueblos, stacked atop each
other like Lego lands constructed by

the creative minds of school children.
escaping east, i lack objective and
soon find myself alone in the
wilderness adjoining Lake Mead,

drawn to the solace of nature. the
unmarked single-lane road stretches
into the expanse, meandering
between mountains and slithering

sideways like the serpent tempting
Jesus in the desert. without notice, the
paved path ends, presenting me with
only a barren, gravel road. do i follow

the path of pebbles and seek
destinations unknown or take the
return road to the splendors of
Sin City and set my soul alight?

the choice seems obvious.

rejecting the temptations of the world,
i proceed down the road less traveled
thru *valleys of fire* and reconnect with
abandoned Anasazi spirits before the

Arrowhead Trial hands me, scorching,
over to I-15 South and back into Las
Vegas. with no reason to sigh, I can
only reply, ROBERT FROST WAS RIGHT.

and *that* has made no difference at all.

Converging

Converging deserts merge, unite, and grab each other by the hands as Set takes roll: Mojave! Sonoran! Great Basin!

Leaving behind Grand Canyon, Red River sweeps the desert and descends on Black Canyon, bringing life! pioneers! farms! to neighboring valleys and basins.

Mesa House Anasazi natives dwell in pueblos manufacture baskets mine salt trade food goods for Four Corners mountain pottery coastal turquoise.

                                        (Life is good.)

Drought arrives.
Crops fail.
Malnutrition reigns.
Abandonment triumphs.

                                        The city is lost.

Time passes. Enter the Mormons.

Religious pilgrims dwell in homes raise cotton operate stores provide food lodging for trailblazers following the Old Arrowhead.

St. Thomas thrives at the junctions of the Muddy and Virgin Rivers where settlers peacefully cohabit with the Southern Paiutes and effectively end the Indian slave trade.

                                        (Life is good.)

Time passes. Enter the Bureau.

Merging deserts converge, unite, and grab hands as Hugh Lord takes roll: Mojave, Sonoran, and Great Basin present and accounted for.

Saying goodbye to Grand Canyon, Colorado River sweeps the desert and descends on Black Canyon only to find Hoover Dam blocking its path.

Water arrives.
Crops fail.
Progress reigns.
Abandonment triumphs.

The city is lost.

The city is lost to those who wait for the river to run dry before crossing, needlessly missing meditative reflections

tendered by the changing bank
rendered by the changing bank.

HOT SEXY GIRLS

the heat takes hold
and melts you from
the inside out (like
little plastic army
men succumbing
to the incandescence
of your sister's easy
bake oven and
metamorphosing into
nothing more than
green globs of
hardened, toxic goo).

forgotten pop-culture
icons from a wholesome
era resurface in an
ill-fated attempt to
reclaim past glories.

like Canadian geese
flying to warmer
climates, flocks of tourists
assemble in intimate
showrooms and fork
over big bucks to
recapture perished past.

neon-colored street walkers
slap stripper cards
against the deck
        shove them in your face
        try their best
        to entice you
        to buy
        HOT SEXY GIRLS.

multi-colored drunken hookers
slap hands
against each other's asses
        shove them in your face
        try their best
        to entice you
        to buy
        HOT SEXY GIRLS
        a drink.

faux alcoves
of Rome
and Venice
manifest
a travesty
of authenticity
resurrecting
man-made illusions
of thousands
of years
of culture
via counterfeit canals
fraudulent fountains
reflect
LED signs
LCD screens
selling all
you can eat
buffets late
nite live
shows.

outside the Flamingo
microcosms of madness
        mimic reality
        increase instant insanity
        multiply mass hysteria.

following advice
Raoul Duke and i
forget folly
ride the crest
of a massive wave
lurching over
las vegas
boulevard

until—
       it bre
            a
               k
                  s

leaving us flying
over dancing clouds
(reeling and swooping)
       knowing
       the entire time
       we had pushed
       our luck
       a bit too far.

i know now that we pushed our luck too far.

The Heart of the Coconut

malapropos palms mirthfully surround Lady Liberty's Las Vegas doppelganger as she distends from the depths of a foot-deep mote

and stands erect as the centerpiece of a comic book Manhattan skyline. wind sweeps psalms of sadness across the façade of

imposter Ellis Island, deflecting the pain of the *TIRED AND POOR* and rejecting the pleas of a *HOMELESS, TEMPEST-TOSSED* woman who grips

with both hands a neatly written cardboard sign that unabashedly broadcasts: *PLEASE HELP. I JUST WANT TO GET HOME TO MY DAUGHTER.*

strip scenes rustle herds of *HUDDLED MASSES* from destination to destination under the guise of American Dreams, while beneath

replica representations of Eifel Tower, Brooklyn Bridge, and Roman Colosseum a labyrinth of dank flood tunnels wreaks *WRETCHED*

REFUGE for hundreds of displaced indigents whose American Reality reeks stagnant water and putrid body waste. but at *SUNSET GATES*

abides my dream: transcending American indifference by standing as an open *GOLDEN DOOR*, glowing as a beacon of freedom, where,

in harmony, you and i *BREATHE FREE*, sharing the world, united in communal exile. in my dream, we share the world in exile as one.

Chasing Ghosts

escalator ascends
from gaming floor
to hotel entrance

metal rolling fire door
blocks access
to 1850

trespassing—
that's just
a misdemeanor

breaking & entering—
that's
a felony

but Gonzo said:
GO STRAIGHT
FOR THE JUGULAR

blocks away
on courthouse steps
i can hear my lawyer say:

AS YOUR ATTORNEY
I ADVISE YOU TO TAKE THE ~~*MESCALINE*~~
STAIRS BACK DOWN AND EXIT

there's
gotta be
another way

or am i just roaming
these ~~Mint~~ Binion escalators
chasing a ghost?

a suicidal ghost with
gun in mouth
phone in hand

~~inspiring~~
expiring
a generation

there's
gotta be
another way

NO
OTHER
WAY—

it's time to let ghosts go
it's time to let sleeping ghosts lie
it's time to quit chasing ghosts

Burning Ocean

A cool front circulates the desert, sending swirling cyclones through the streets of suburban Summerlin.

Opposition Jupiter Optimus Maximus dominates the nighttime sky, passing judgment on the earthly realm and swiftly sending jovial justice to those seeking verisimilitude.

Enter Cassiopeia—circling, circling, circling—swimming through the celestial sphere on her throne of torture, upside down half her life: a suspended symbol of her own vanity, vanishing by dawn's early light.

Daylight defeats darkness as Ra rises over the valley, revealing Red Rock Canyon and painting a deep, midnight-blue empyrean sky in my western backyard.

I have not slept in what seems like weeks and fear that I am losing touch with reality.

In this town, distinguishing between fantasy and reality is already difficult enough.

My mind will not stop.
   Thoughts arise like solar flares escaping the surface of the sun.

What am I doing in the desert?

Did I really leave life behind?
   Or had life left me behind long ago?

And where the fuck did I park *The Lincoln*?

The day is new and the future unwritten; but the places I have been, etched on the Internet for electronic eternity, already seem like a forgotten memory from another lifetime.

Time rears its relative head, and I jump a beam of light,
   transporting myself through a quantum tunnel back to the past.

260 million years ago, on the same spot I just departed, I am on
   an island, sitting on the beach, watching the birth of the Late
   Permian sun over the cold, thawing ocean.

The world is changing.
   Boulder is burning.

California is combusting.
   Elvis' soul is on fire.

Viva Las Vegas!
   Viva, Las Vegas.

Somewhere

tick tock.
tick tock.

seconds steal time,
hawking them at

the universal pawn
shop of special

relativity where
heaven is a FAIRY

STORY for those
afraid of the dark.

my beam of light
drops me off—

somewhere ...

He Ain't Heavy; He's My Brother

Insomnia, my new best friend, keeps me company as another novel day arrives into my timeless world. *The Lincoln*, feeling refreshed after overcoming a bout of flat tire, begs to be driven.

We cruise down *The 515* with no destination in mind, and before I realize it, she has taken me downtown.

The newly restored neon signs of what is now called *The Fremont Street Experience* attempt to revivify *Glitter Gulch*, the western end of Fremont Street seen in nearly every movie or television show that wants to capture the lights of Las Vegas.

Now, a giant canopy covers the street, which is shut off to vehicular traffic, and pedestrians move from casino to casino under the safety of a covered, four-block-long open-air shopping mall, complete with bright lights and Viva Vision LED show.

While carelessly wandering past the Four Queens and attempting to ascertain what cosmic event of unparalleled importance drew me here, I spot an African-American man favoring a well-defined limp. He makes eye contact with me and slowly approaches.

I have two choices: (1) quickly flee across Casino Center Boulevard like an ignorant racist and ditch him in a crowd of people; or (2) wait like a caring, empathetic human being and engage him in conversation.

Allow me to present Marine Staff Sergeant Tony (he asked me to redact his last name). Nine years ago, Sgt. Tony lived a *normal* life with his girlfriend in Wichita, Kansas. Today, he refuses to contact her, afraid that he is going to "choke her out."

Inspired by the "heroism and patriotism" of the New York Fire Department on 11 September 2001, Sgt. Tony immediately enlisted in the Marines and was deployed to Iraq as part of the first wave of the 2003 invasion.

Sporting barely a day's worth of stubble on his face and a freshly shaved head, it is hard to tell that Sgt. Tony has been on the streets, sleeping in bathrooms and bathing in sinks, since his discharge from the hospital six days ago after going into insulin shock.

"I was just walking around, minding my own business, and my vision goes out," he says with a certain uneasiness in his voice. "Then a SWAT team shows up and takes me down. I woke up in the hospital … had no idea I'm diabetic."

The thirty-six year old vet's face is hardened and worn, displaying lines of life usually only apparent in someone twice his age, and his voice carries the angry wisdom of a man who has experienced too much pain for a single lifetime: "People roll dice, a thousand dollars a roll. Tip a girl with fake titties a hundred bucks, but they won't buy a vet a cup a coffee."

While on patrol in Afghanistan in 2008, an IED exploded near Sgt. Tony's Humvee, shrapnel struck his head, and he lost his left eye. An empty, collapsed socket is all that remains. "I came out here to Vegas to go to Nellis to get my eye fixed," he says with a newly discovered sense of confidence. "I'm not leaving 'til the mission's complete."

But Sgt. Tony's mission seems futile at this point. The maxillofacial surgeons at Nellis Air Force Base's 114-bed medical treatment facility, run in a joint venture with the Department of Veterans Affairs, refuse to operate until his diabetes are under control.

Fresh diabetes diagnosis (and homelessness) aside, Sgt. Tony's greatest challenge, however, seems to be overcoming mental illness. He says that when he returned home from his third tour in Afghanistan he spent four months in a psych ward and received no therapy or counseling. "They asked me if I heard voices. I said, 'Sometimes,'" he admits as he looks over his shoulder and then hides his face from a passing security guard.

"They told me I was bipolar and had Post-Traumatic Stress Disorder," he continues after a moment. "Hell, I'm schizophrenic."

Doctors prescribed him a cocktail of psychotropic drugs: Lithium, Zoloft, Seroquel, and Thorazine. Sgt. Tony no longer takes his meds and is depressed and suicidal.

He says his bronze star and two purple hearts mean nothing to him. "It's not about those symbols. I love this country and would do it all over again," Sgt. Tony expresses with pride. "But I hate the government and just want my eye back."

The sun slowly rises over the canopy of Fremont Street, and the neon lights flicker no more. Sgt. Tony hobbles off into the distance, a shadow of his previous self and a hidden casualty of the Iraq and Afghan wars. A Musak version of the Beatle's *Penny Lane* plays over the loudspeakers.

I sit, and meanwhile back.
I sit, and meanwhile ...

Melody #87

wild-eyed hipsters awake rapidly (cold and wet), roll out of bed
furiously, and start the day's quest (reacting), futilely navigating

through self-constructed mazes of exile, driven to backstreet
black market fixes and simultaneously descending upon locked-

door rooms of privacy, waiting patiently in the queue for the
next rides on soiled, solitary magic mattresses that float

incandescently off hardwood floors of hope, guided blindly by
anxious Aladdins who serve dreams within dreams and hearken

Delphi for elucidation while traveling backward in ecstasy,
tantric trips of transcendental proportions fabricate reality and

progenerate mystifying reflections ricocheting violently off
broken mirrors of perception, two fists of fury swoop down like

a tornado—stabbing, omitting, forgetting—and skate
spellbound to lands of imprisoned fantasy, glorious

manipulation without reprieve but owning no guilt like a little
girl blaming her brother after breaking his toy car, couch surfers

riding borrowed waves stolen from brothers left standing at the
shore, alone, destined to watch grains of microscopic sand slip

through fingers like Gibsons disappearing into a black hole of
selfish desire where painful truths discover sidewalk's end, a

lonely place where cruelness supersedes kindness and
unknown adversaries arise, leaving behind martyrs that befall

disappeared daemons while spirits sit idly on parole, watching
drops of dignity float away on rainbowed balloons expanding

into the clouds, converging with Icarus, and plummeting into
the sea with shattered memories and forgotten dreams that

echo broken melodies, crying out from depths of doubt and
resurrecting life with every wave that crashes into the shore.

forgotten memories recall shattered dreams,
reborn when each wave reaches the shore ...

Dizzy Math (The Thizz of Nature)

My beam of light returns me to the desert, an oasis:
   Calico Basin's saltgrass meadow, thriving in homeostasis.

Natural springs emerge from the base of sandstone cliffs,
   petrified sand dunes decorated with native petroglyphs.

Southern Paiutes displaced by the Homestead Act of '62;
   39,000 square miles stolen without further review.

Aboriginal homelands redistributed to settlers;
   a barren reservation, the gift to tribal elders.

Then, in 1938, the Small Tract Act passed;
   free fertile land for all, the Dust Bowl was aghast.

But now, the BLM wants the real estate back,
   paying 700 grand per acre or 3.5 million for each tract.

That's a hell of a lot more than they paid our Piaute brethren;
   a 1965 court judgment awarded 2 bucks an acre for Calico Basin.

Now all these numbers are making me dizzy;
   it's time to forget myself and drop Tu-weap's ecstasy.

Rollin from acre to acre;
   rollin on the *thizz* of nature.

Dark Ages

Every home in Arizona is the same color: desert sand. Rust colored rocks replace green grass and take root in miniscule yards, painting a desaturated suburban landscape reminiscent of a 1950s black & white sitcom sponsored by Phillip Morris.

Evangelical Republicans—Tea Party favorites—seek to replace the color and diversity of America with a parochial uniformity similarly found in Southwestern sprawl and the sanitized, *wholesome* fantasy of the Golden Age of Television.

   turn off your TV
   america
   awake

(from your slumbers of amnesia)

   bury Tea Party ideals
   in the cemetery
   of our checkered past

(let us return not to the Dark Ages)

The Race

The checkered flag rapidly drops, signaling the start of today's race for survival.

Commuters travel east on Charleston, fleeing suburbs' safety for the *security* of Strip employment, where the balance of life hangs from a tiny thread dangling from the top of the Stratosphere.

The state of the economy—rising unemployment, debt, foreclosures, and evictions—stands as the biggest threat to the mental health of the valley community and contributes to the highest suicide rate in the nation, nearly twice as high as the rest of the country.

It is easy to see why euthanized apparitions stayed only three days and in order to survive needed a trunkload of drugs that LOOKED LIKE A MOBILE POLICE NARCOTICS LAB.

Once the Disney-like magic of the marketing wears off and the allure of the bright lights fades to day, the city kidnaps and her residents cling to the last remnants of life, abiding like a swatted fly whose broken left wing furiously flickers until it realizes the gift of flight is gone.

I long for life outside the manufactured realities of the Las Vegas Boulevard of Broken Dreams.

I long for the real streets of Rome, where in a bar beneath the remains of the Colosseum an Italian man plays guitar and sings in broken English *Light My Fire*—not a faux Coliseum where Cher executes stale pop to sell-out crowds paying five-hundred a head.

I long for the real cuisine of Venice, where family-owned restaurants serve home-cooked meals and house-wines from local vineries—not mass produced all-you-can-eat casino buffets sitting atop copied canals.

I long for the real perfume of Lower Manhattan and my daily stroll from Midtown skyscrapers to a Chelsea office overlooking the Hudson—not a roller coaster ride around a replica Metropolis skyline lifted from a post World War II Superman comic.

I long for the real flavor of the Pacific's salt-water on my tongue—not the essence emanating from the tears of salt-water sweat rolling down my fraying face: hemorrhaging perspiration courtesy the intense, ardent desert.

I long for the open air of the road and the freedom of not knowing where each day will take me.

My nomadic spirit cannot sit still.

The sirens sing songs of hope, joyously luring my return to the road.

>   Goodbye Las Vegas.
>   Goodbye Hoover Dam.
>   Goodbye night-time ninety-four.
>   Hello early-morning forty-seven.
>   Hello Route-66.
>   Hello Flagstaff.

THE TRUTH (FROM A HOTEL ROOM IN FLAGSTAFF)

THE SETUP—
Former President Jimmy Carter on Larry King Live:
A LOT OF GULLIBLE FOLKS IN THE UNITED STATES ACTUALLY BELIEVE WHAT FOX PUTS FORWARD AS FACTS WHEN MOST OF IT IS JUST COMPLETE DISTORTIONS ... THERE HAS BEEN A DELIBERATE EFFORT— AGAIN, REFERRING TO FOX BROADCASTING—TO INJECT THE RACE ISSUE INTO IT.

Fox *News* commentator Bill O'Reilly replied:
SO IT SEEMS MR. CARTER IS NOT TELLING THE TRUTH, AND IT IS BENEATH A FORMER PRESIDENT TO ACCUSE FNC OF INJECTING RACE INTO THE POLITICAL PROCESS AS CARTER DOES. CARTER CAN SIMPLY NOT BACK UP WHAT HE SAYS ...

THE TRUTH—
Fox *News* commentator Glenn Beck professed:
THIS PRESIDENT HAS EXPOSED HIMSELF AS A GUY, OVER AND OVER AND OVER AGAIN, WHO HAS A DEEP-SEATED HATRED FOR WHITE PEOPLE ... OBAMA HAS A PROBLEM. THIS GUY IS, I BELIEVE, A RACIST.

News Corp CEO Rupert Murdoch defended:
ON THE RACIST THING, THAT CAUSED A GRILLING. BUT OBAMA DID MAKE A VERY RACIST COMMENT. AHHH ... ABOUT, YOU KNOW, BLACKS AND WHITES AND SO ON ... AND UM ... IF YOU ACTUALLY ASSESS WHAT BECK WAS TALKING ABOUT, HE WAS RIGHT.

THE SOLUTION—
FucK Bill O'Reilly.
fUcK Glenn Beck.
FuCk Rupert Murdoch.
fUCk Fox.
FUCK RACISM.

Becoming

After a restless night's sleep, I awoke this morning ready to drive, drive, drive.

My first destination: Meteor Crater, the site of an asteroid impact around 50,000 years ago—or about 40,000 years before Homo sapiens first migrated from Asia to the region.

BUT AN ASTEROID STRIKE COULD NOT HAVE OCCURRED THAT LONG AGO SINCE THE EARTH IS LESS THAN 10,000 YEARS OLD, a belief shared by 44 percent of Americans according to a 2008 Gallup poll.

Until 1543, a geocentric model of the universe prevailed as science. Today, 26 percent of Americans still believe that the sun revolves around the earth.

The Catholic Church, in 1633, convicted Galileo Galilei of heresy for advocating Copernicus' heliocentric model of the solar system. He spent the remainder of his life under house arrest.

> John Lennon had it wrong. God, in fact, is a concept that enables people to escape the truth. I shall say it again. God is a concept that enables people to escape the truth.

> Jesus said, THE TRUTH WILL SET YOU FREE, unless you are Galileo of course.

Refusing to pay $15 to see the mile in diameter hole in the ground, I return to Interstate-40 East.

Magnificent clouds dance in unison across the sky until the Cholla Power Plant emerges and delivers clouds of coal combustion waste that emit carbon and sulfur dioxides into the sky, crocheting afghans of surging smog.

As I cross into New Mexico, the heavens rip open, and Navajo spirits dump divine tears of rain, furiously pelting the purlieu.

Visibility drops to thirty-feet for the next four hundred miles. But I welcome the cleansing power of the rain.

> Christianity does not encourage its adherents to seek spiritual cleansing through truth, only through repentance of *sin*.
>
> Christianity seeks definition through absolutes and dualities: right and wrong, good and evil, heaven and hell, God and Satan.
>
> Christianity, thereby, creates for its followers a black & white worldview, which wrongfully judges and condemns what lies outside its parochial realm of perception.
>
> But the world is not black & white. And one's perceptions should not be the sole gauge used in determining one's reality.

I used to live as if I were a surfer riding a wave: reacting to life's obstacles and challenges instead of overcoming life's obstacles and challenges by acting.

But I no longer want to *be* the surfer riding a wave.
I want, I long, to *be*come the wave.

Life is not *being*.
Life is *becoming*.

I *am* becoming.

Turn Around

my fingers reek of raw leather,
as if i've been wearing baseball

batting gloves on both my hands
for the last three days. while this

possibility intrigues me, it seems
both impractical and highly unlikely

that i would engage in such a behavior.
i surmise a more logical explanation

for my freshly found odor: *The Lincoln's*
new, genuine pleather steering wheel

cover. the dual-lane highway is not the
most efficient mode of progress, but the

lack of traffic on US-56 along the Santa
Fe Trail through New Mexico, Oklahoma,

and Kansas allows me escape into a world
of translucent thought. cerulean skies cosset

careless cumulus clouds, cavorting with
Nephelai and creating an insurmountable

barrier between the firmament and
space-time continuum. despite my

repeated attempts to capture a floating
piece of cotton candy and soar away, the

wheels of *The Lincoln* remain glued to the
road and my body strapped to her front seat.

every fifty miles, or so, a small town
—a grain elevator and a water tower—

springs from the horizon. a community
of people must exist somewhere nearby,

but from the road, the prospect of thriving
life appears elusive. for the first time in

months, i am bewildered and insouciant,
void of emotion, and lack the vocabulary

to express my thoughts. we waste precious
time walking in circles, desperately grabbing

for what we think we *want*—that elusive
fixation forever dangling in front of us like

a hypnotist's gold-plated pocketwatch—
forgetting the entire time to grab a glance

and see that what we really *need* walks
patiently behind us with outstretched arms.

check your six before Time slips away.
check your six before it's too late.

)E-M-O-H(

                                                                                              Home—

        a place to rest your
head a pillow a warm
bed the backseat of a
car a rock under that bright
star seen through half-cracked front windows a dark waning
moon darting back and forth and forth and back across the
lagoon eyes envision curiosities coming and going with
        guitar in hand a dream:

        blue dirt visions of rose highways
painting a morphined sunbeam
carrying picasso
tripping in spite of everything
singing sounds (no more sounds) of engines
humming winds
whipping tiny blades of grass
growing green leaves
turning brown
falling to the ground prometheus unbound in a ten % solution
grifting spellbound sherlock
pilfering watson (no more)
waiting at home in motionless atrophy
lacking gravity
rebelling then floating
        (spontaneously)

        down algae laden alleys of
        down algae laden baggies of
        down algae laden valleys ghandi does dilly with e.e.

        progress stalls silence stonewalls poxy speedballs
sprawling A.W.O.L
calling nepal mauling
        (sol's cure-all)
                                          —nepal calls sol's cure-all

Hiatus: of

words flow freely from fingertips to laptop keyboards transcribing
   thoughts of

reflections intimations without
   punctuation of

previously trapped deep in the
   recesses of

overdrive receptors sending swirling
   signals of

electrical current from shadowy
   chasms of

frozen spheres to void-less sweet
   stars of

eternal light
   apparitions of

forever endeavoring in accord with stringed dimensions born
   free of

defective (intelligently) designed intellectual
   idioms of

delicate and vicious descent upon
   screens of

illumination burning in harmony with media's etched
   contemplations of

vomited didactical dialects spewing
   diarrhea of

sages born and eyewitnesses
   unborn of

mentally digested constipated
   feelings of

current powering solared idyllic
   notions of

eastward motion in
   search of

oceans atlantic and cities secluded from dormant fault
   lines of

restrained puissance by scripture's sacred
   belts of

parochial new
   testaments of

white stripes selling chuck
   taylors of

innocent criminals capitulating to cadillac's
   cash of

modest mice floating on stars' satellite
   systems of

cake cutting slices into apple's
   core of

(no more)
   dreams of

lennon's imagination bombarding mainstreaming
   minds of

boomers' babies infantilized consumers shelled by nuclear
    discharges of

one party polity and plutocracy fashioning
    attitudes of

chasing caesar's dead presidents and huffing vitriolic
    granules of

soundbites kilobytes dust
    mites of

infected ratiocination inducing
    inhalation of

faculty and lungs filled to
    capacity of

digested regurgitated exhaled inertia superseding supplanted
    seeds of

sowers yore saving
    secrets of

straight-dope seekers searching for freely flowing transcribed
    words of

returned
    thoughts of

reflected congregating overcome
    banks of

crashing into bathed and waxed
    lincolns of

(breakingdentingsmashingcracking) taillight eternal raving into
    intimations of

free dimensions void-less apparitions forever in accord within
　imaginations of

projected possibilities on
　screens of

dreams from fingertips to laptop
　keyboards of

dreams to
　screens of

idyllic
　streams of
　consciousness of
　ideas of
　inspiration of

hypnotizing
　lines of

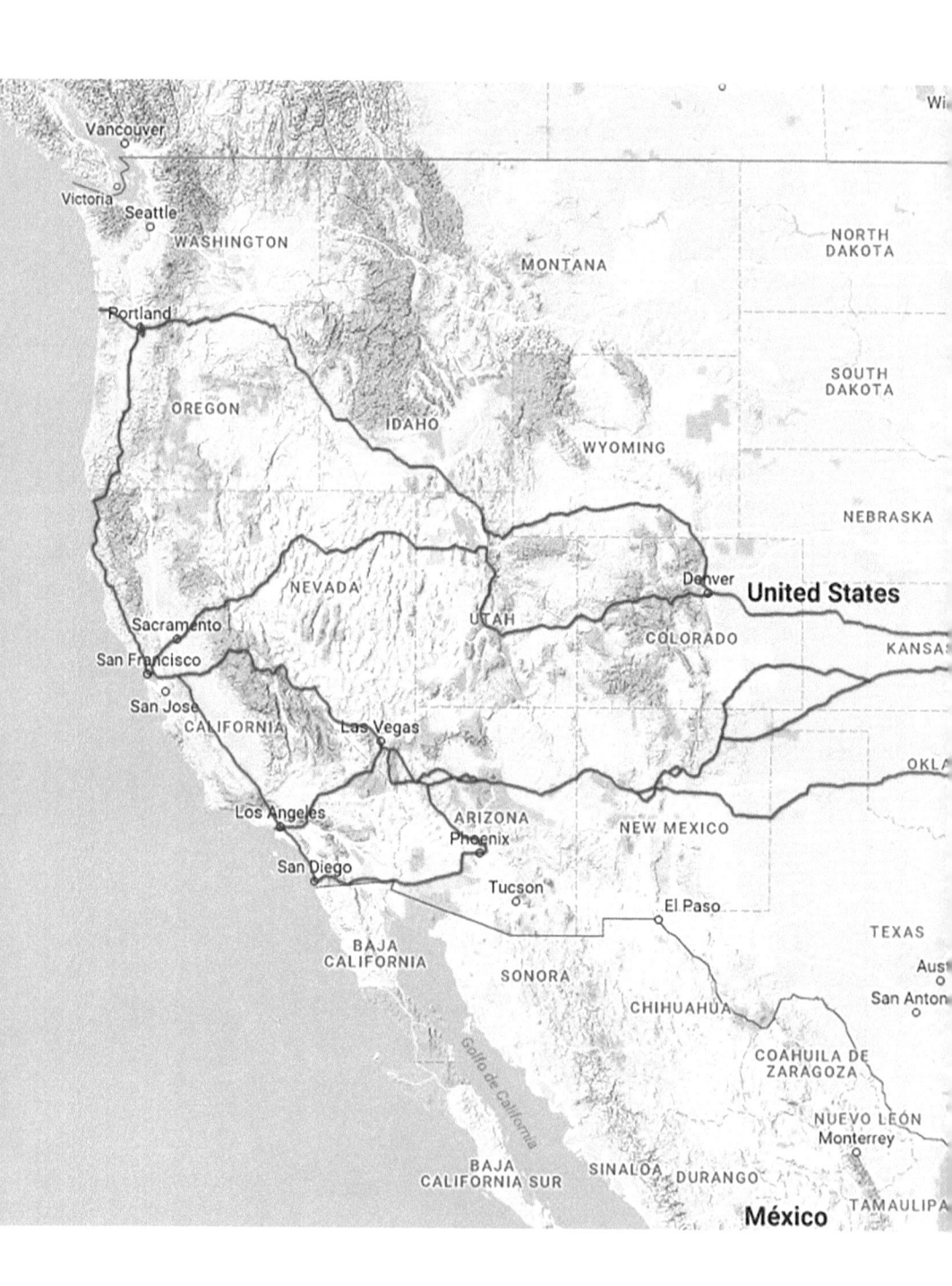

August 2010 — July 2011

j.d.tulloch is a writer, filmmaker, and social activist. He is the founder of 39 West Press and has worked in broadcast radio and for the management team of the late Godfather of Soul, James Brown.

www.ingramcontent.com/pod-product-compliance
Lightning Source LLC
Chambersburg PA
CBHW050911300426

44111CB00010B/1474